The Beauty of Growth

POEMS BY
TIA GEORGES

MILTON & HUGO L.L.C.
4407 Park Ave., Suite 5
Union City, NJ 07087, USA

Website: *www. miltonandhugo.com*
Hotline: *1- 888-778-0033*
Email: *info@miltonandhugo.com*

Ordering Information:
Quantity sales. Special discounts are granted to corporations, associations, and other organizations. For more information on these discounts, please reach out to the publisher using the contact information provided above.

Library of Congress Control Number: 2024926445
ISBN-13:   979-8-89285-401-6   [Paperback Edition]
                 979-8-89285-400-9   [Hardback Edition]
                 979-8-89285-399-6   [Digital Edition]

Rev. date: 12/09/2024

in loving memory
of the ones I've lost

dedicated to
my friends and family

Contents

Before you,
I never understood the idea
that a person could be a home.

For a home is a physical place
or is that a house,
simply made of four walls and a roof
missing the tenderness of love.

A love I never felt.

You offer me a safety
of which I've never known
by simply becoming my home.
A sanctuary from the troubles
and the pain I endure.

My heart was barred and guarded
against those who wished to hold her
and no matter how hard I pushed,

you pushed back

against the pain
against the trauma
against my inability to love myself

and you loved me.

You showed me the beauty
of that special kind of love
you find within a *home*.

~ a house is not a home

you would point out my insecurities
and claim they were your favorite
I shied away
when you put the attention on me
I would never believe the compliments I received

despite my unwillingness
you took the time
to unravel each knotted insecurity living in my head
until I was sitting there
letting the strings slip through my fingers

the longer I looked at them
falling towards nothing
the more they began to knot
but you didn't reach for the scissors

you reached for my hand

~ side by side

I shall find you again
as I always have
my body may be left behind
but my soul is what goes searching for yours
I will look
until I find you
wherever that may be
whenever that may be
we are bound together

~ soul tied

I never believed I'd find a love like this
from the moment you walked in
I've felt nothing but pure bliss.

When we're with one another
it's as though the stars align
and for me there is no other.

Hardships will appear
for relationships take work
yet I have no fear.

Safety is what I offer you,
a love that will never waiver, bend, or break
a future we didn't believe could be true.

So here I stand, my love
ready to fight for you
when push comes to shove.

~ steady

people always told me
don't go looking for love
it'll come when it's meant to

so after a while of being let down
and always getting hurt
I started questioning if it was true

but the moment we met
I felt something different

the thought never truly settled

yet
I felt like maybe
it finally came for me too

~ fate

I remember the way my hand felt
like it was lit ablaze
the first time she grabbed it
interlocking our fingers
and letting our hands rest beside us
the soft smile growing on my face
her hand felt like an anchor
keeping me tethered

I remember the way she looked at me
the curiosity and interest shining in her eyes
before my hands rested on her soft skin
and pulled her closer
the fireworks that people experience
was a mere myth
before our lips connected

I remember the way my heart fluttered
against the cage of bone it was enclosed in
the moment we made a soft promise
to grow together
for as long as the other would allow

those three little words
set my mind ablaze
and my body felt as light as air

~ engraved

as
the
    rain
        falls
I sit there, soaked to the bone
encompassed by your love,
feeling as though I'm no longer alone

as
    the
rain
    falls
we lay by the fire,
wondering how we got so lucky,
and I know our love will never expire

as
the
    rain
  falls
when our hair has turned gray
and wrinkles cover our skin
life has turned out better than okay

~ *the ticking of life*

the needle pricked my skin
marking me with ink
the relief of the pain
throbbed on my arm
back and forth
back and forth
hours upon hours
sitting there
waiting for the art to help me feel
complete
the beauty of the art settled on
my arm

felt heavy
with the weight of her head
laying side by side
her dark orbs full of light
looking up at me
with a tenderness
I didn't even know existed
there was a magnetism
that encompassed her
drawing me in
eyes closed, blind to her
beauty
the feeling of us
finally embracing
was unlike a sweetness
I've ever known

when I was learning Arabic
I always used to get
far and sweet confused
for the sweetness I crave
is always too far for me to reach
but is that not what makes it sweeter?
The inability to have it
makes me want it more

~ tenderness

the first time we locked eyes
was the moment I knew
you were meant for me

after all that's been done
fragments of my heart
are all that's left

for you, I gave them all up
I turned a blind eye
and despite it all
I began to lose you
until I was grasping

at
            nothing
                        but

                                                air

the last time we locked eyes
was the moment I knew
you were meant for another

yet, I'd let you break my heart again

you tell me I can't
because maybe,
just maybe

it will be different
with someone new

~ and I've just begun to heal

you pulled on my strings
until I was nothing
but a shell of my former self

you made me

d	s	l	t	t
a	p	a	h	r
n	e	u	i	u
c	a	g	n	s
e	k	h	k	t

I knew it was bound to happen
for all the late nights were far too perfect

the cutting of my strings
left me with a feeling of emptiness
that spread throughout my body

from the top of my head
to the tips of my toes
a piece of me was missing
the moment you decided

I wasn't enough

~ puppeteer

13

on the nights my mind
seems to run nonstop,
I feel as though I'm a prisoner confined
unable to bring my thoughts to a full stop

on the days we don't talk,
I feel my doubts start to seep in
sitting here at 4AM, staring at the clock,
my reassurance begins to wear thin

lovers is what we called each other
but as our relationship grew,
I realized that you've always had another
one that could see right through you

looking back on the memories we've shared,
the tears broke through
because I truly believed you cared,
but now I know what's true

throughout my life,
the one I thought would always be by my side,
was the one actually holding the knife

a lesson presented itself
through your betrayal

~ I can only ever count on myself

the pain
of feeling like I'm a part of some game
cannot be put into words

they always say
it will happen when you least expect it
but what if I do expect it?

expect it to never happen

this game has a hold on us all
I shall play no more
for I have had enough

enough

I wish I was enough

~ single player

you're stuck in a skin that isn't yours
changing who you are
just to survive

acceptance

support

love

you catch a glimpse of them
through others, but you,
you'll never experience them firsthand

the walls are closing in
with every breath
through a mouth that isn't yours

~ chameleon

Putting others first
is like the air you breathe.
Yet somehow, you don't see yourself suffocating.

Sure.

Of course.

Why not?

Are words engraved into your head,
but one is missing, is it not?

It's always there,
dancing on the tip of your tongue,
but too shy to ever come out.

Just one more favor?

No

- problem.

~ people pleaser

I remember the way the sand burned our feet
as we ran towards the water
the salty air filling our nostrils
as the sun beat down on our shoulders and face

I remember the way her fingers, covered in rings, slipped between
mine
as we walked past the yellow and green playground we grew up in

I remember the way my sister and I bounded towards the
Christmas tree
pulling along our groggy parents
bouncing with excitement as we saw the empty plate of Christmas
cookies

I remember the way she used to hit me in the arm
every time she spotted an out of state license plate
music blasting as we cruised on the freeway

I remember the way she looked at me when I shared a piece of
myself
the disappointment evident in the way her shoulders sagged
fearing how people would speak about her
for the kind of daughter she raised

I remember the way a mix of fear and anxiety coursed through my body
as I saw the flashing red and blue lights behind me, traffic zipping by
the time slowly ticking down to when I was supposed to be at work

I remember the way it felt like life stopped and it was all just a nightmare
the faint sounds of my mom and dad crying barely registering in my mind
the earlier feeling of the warmth of the blanket now foreign and nonexistent

I remember the way my grandpa looked at me,
his proud smile lighting up his soft features as I placed down the last card
his laugh still echoing in my ears as he called for a rematch every time

I remember the moments that turned me into who I am

~ press rewind

stuck
the words in my throat
tried to claw their way through
the despair gripped my heart
its claws piercing the veins
keeping me alive

is there even a point anymore?

regardless of the quality of our lives
we are not discriminated against in death

~ the bigger picture

No.

The hardest part is saying no.
Everyone keeps asking, but my answer never changes.

I lost a best friend
and with that loss, I began to lose myself.

My 'no' began to change.
No turned to maybe
and maybe turned to sure.

Something I always swore off
now calls to me
like a neon sign.

What's the worst that could happen?
I had never wanted to find out.

No.

Are you sure you don't want to try?
Over time, my endurance has begun to wane,
like sediment being tormented by a river.

Maybe.

When you left, so did my resolve.

Sure.

~ peer pressure

my mom wraps the blanket around my shoulders
each time I start shaking
trying to protect me from the cold
but what she doesn't know
is my body does not tremble from the cold
that numbs my fingers
or raise goosebumps along my arm

I tremble from the fear
of knowing what's coming next

how am I supposed to shatter her image
of the perfect daughter
she's spent half her life raising
simply to be able to live my own

~ *fear leads to change*

my past self
had to conceal herself
from those she loved the most

what hurts is she lost a part of herself
hiding who she was for so long
that I didn't recognize her
when she wasn't hiding anymore

what hurts is she lost a relationship
with the people who gave her life
when I finally decided
I was going to live it

I see my younger self standing there
bewildered and scared

if I could, I would walk right up to her
and tell her:
the ones who truly love you
will not stop loving you

if I could, I would walk right up to her
and tell her:
she's not meant to be
alone in this world

if I could, I would walk right up to her
and tell her:
her life does not dictate another's happiness
her life is her own to live

if I could, I would walk right up to her
and tell her:
she is loved
she has always been loved
she will be loved
by someone she calls home

~ *if only*

sitting under a sky of darkness
one woman battles herself

the expectations that society inflicts on her
turn her into someone she doesn't recognize

pieces of her heart have been cut out
as she loses herself
to the box society shoves her in

connected to the pain
was a certain strength
the strength from her culture
kept her whole

the pain of the inability to create
life
weighed on her

it kept her angry
it kept her alive

the pain turned her into who she is

~ through it all

an old man bends over a bouquet of pink tulips

>   Why would her mom ask?
>   Ask about me
>   Why would her mom ask?
>   We didn't
>   We couldn't
>   We were careful

a little girl in yellow
zips past me
rushing towards the ice cream
with her mom in tow

>   It'll be my fault
>   I know   She said
>   It won't happen
>   How is she sure?
>   Why would her mom ask?

the wheel squeaks as I push
the cart down the pet supply aisle

>   Is she scared?
>   Scared of her mom finding out?
>   What if her parents   don't   agree?
>   My mom doesn't like
>   How her parents don't know
>   She's worried about me
>   We're careful

the young woman reaches over
grabbing a bag of hot cheetos
and ranch doritos

What if she's bored?
What if she gets bored?
What if I'm too much?
What if?
What if?
What if?
What if?

I reach for a box of strawberries,
the cool plastic pressing against my fingers

There's no way her mom will find out
She doesn't
She wouldn't
She couldn't
But
Why would her mom ask?
Unless she already knows

I

look

down

at

the

red

carnations

staining my hands.

~ bleeding

it's no lie
to be loved is one of the greatest feelings
but how can you love another
if you don't love yourself

~ to be seen is to be loved

what they don't tell you about love
is that the hurt created by a broken heart
is unlike any other

so while you may feel like life's joys have become vast
don't forget about the pain
that comes with entrusting your heart in someone else's hands
if they choose to hold it too tightly

~ *suffocating*

I tried to follow in your footsteps
but   the   tracks   had   faded

living my life to meet your expectations
has left me confused and alone

I tried to follow in your footsteps
but you had stopped walking
leaving me to pick up the pieces
you left behind

piece by piece they click into place
creating a broken picture

since I am unable to fix myself
I must settle for the incomplete puzzle
resting within my hands

~ dead end

a fatal flaw for some
an identity for others

pride

~ two sides of the same coin

a pile of bricks rests upon your chest
weighing you down
it's almost as if you're drowning
day by day they say
but what they don't know
is that for you,
it's more like

s e c o n d

by

s e c o n d

~ *responsibilities*

the artwork that lives on their skin
tells of a story
they keep hidden within

the thought has crossed their mind
and foolish they thought they were
but oh how could they have been so blind

one small drawing unites all
those who have shared the experience
they never wish to recall

the drawing of Medusa's head
connects those who share the burden
and have to live with its effect

now we owe ourselves the duty
of living despite the pain
and understanding the tattooed beauty

~ universal

the nights where I'm left alone
will always be the hardest
seeing as that's the only time
you can invade my mind

looking at old photos of you
and realizing you're never coming back
breaks my heart in ways I didn't know existed

I can feel the tears building
against my hazel walls
and no matter how much mortar I use to seal them
they break like glass

we would never talk about death growing up
but it seems that's all that consumes my thoughts
ever since you left this world
on a search of a new adventure

I've been left drowning

~ in the thought of you

by your side
is where I'll stay
with those auburn eyes
staring back at me
I know there's no place else
I could call home

every memory we've created
has more value within my heart
than riches ever could

I'll be gentle
I won't break your trust
I'll remind you each day
of what you mean to me

so deep in love
I forgot what life looked like before

forever is how long I'll love you

~ I pinky promise

When you first walked into the room
I was captivated by your smile
Like no other, you had me hooked
Left me wondering if our paths would intertwine.

Your chocolate colored eyes locked on mine
Oddly enough, that's when I knew you were
Unapologetically unique.

Before I knew it, the day I was waiting for had come
Every soft touch and stolen glance had me falling harder.

Morning through night, we would talk
Yet it never seemed like enough.

Genuine feelings are all I have for you.
In your arms I feel safe, so I promise I will
Respect the entirety of who you are
Laughing with you brings me a joy unlike any other
For your laugh makes my heart beat faster and I
Realize that I would never want to stop hearing it fall from your lips
I like giving you butterflies and seeing you get shy,
Especially when you bury your face in my shoulder, so please
Never hide your emotions because you're it for me, and I know it's
Daunting, but by your side is where I'm meant to be.

~ hidden meanings

I loved you
in the same way
I wished I loved myself

but I guess it took loving you
to finally notice the lack of love
I gave to myself

~ *is it better to have loved and lost?*

I relied on you
to make me happy
but how could you
if you weren't

you relied on me
to make you feel seen
but how could I
if I lived in the shadows

we relied on each other
to feel complete
but losing you made me realize
I couldn't help another
before I helped myself

I had to let you go

~ learning how to love me

you went searching
for the grass that was greener
on the other   side

                          I hope you found what you were looking for
                                but don't expect me to wait around
                                      until you decide to come
back

I deserve flowers too.

~ *take care of your garden*

when I look back
at the memories of you,
I do feel pain

pain at the loss
of what we had

pain at the loss
of who I was
before we met

pain at the loss
of what could have been

but despite it all
I thank you
for the growth you've helped me achieve
even if the love has disappeared

~ flowers after rain

when I pushed you
to give me the reassurance I needed
maybe you shouldn't have

you gave me that reassurance
despite knowing it didn't hold true

and that hurt more
than any lack of reassurance ever could

~ *don't waste your breath*

I lied to myself with the idea of who I thought you were
after you betrayed me
I still stayed
because I loved you

or did I love the idea of who I thought you were

while I did see you
I never saw you for who you've become
in the beginning, you put on a mask
and slowly, you began to remove it
until I couldn't differentiate
which version was real

~ rose colored glasses

you don't have to pretend
that you're fine
if you feel like you're not
humans rely on companionship
we group together
the way animals do
yet we claim to be independent

you don't have to pretend
that you're okay
if your world is breaking apart
you're not weak when asking for help
allow yourself to rely on others
in the way you allow others to rely on you

~ buoy in the ocean

I loved you
with every fiber of my being
with every beat of my heart
with every breath

and now, I know
there will be no other
that I could love the same

but maybe it's better that way
since I didn't have enough
space to love myself in the end

~ *clear cache*

I fucked up.

I respected you more
than the woman staring back at me
when I looked in the mirror

she didn't deserve
what you put her through
she didn't deserve
what I put her through

I was dumb
I was naive
I was blind

I was in love.

Love is terrifying
but I had the courage

to walk away

and finally
put *her* first

~ don't fear the unknown

the pain that washed over me
when you chose her
brought me to my knees

I chose you
over even myself

that's where I went wrong
so I took the time to heal

it didn't take as long as people claimed
but that was because you had left
through your own desires

after all, if they wanted to
they would

~ *mismatched priorities*

I changed
to love you
in a way that wasn't suffocating

I waited

for you to change
to love me

but no matter how long I stood there
you were set in your ways
unphased by the pain you caused

so as the leaves wither and fall
from the trees that are covered in frost
and the flowers bloom
under the warmth of the sun

I realized

~ even seasons change

maybe I was put in your life
to show you what true unconditional love was
and you were put in mine
to show me how to love myself

~ you were a lesson I had to learn

I sit here night after night
believing I'm not allowing myself to heal
by thinking about the past we shared
but it's not the past we shared that I grieve

it's the future we could have had
the one I created
within the confines of my own mind

but the future I created
was made with the version of you
that I fell in love with
not the version of you
I broke myself to stay with

I will continue to allow myself to grieve
but I won't allow it to be for you anymore

~ *you've wasted enough of my time*

you sit there wondering
where you went wrong
if there was anything you could've done differently

I'm here to tell you that there wasn't

there wasn't anything you could change
because it wasn't your responsibility
to fight for the relationship
if you were the only one fighting

it's unfair

it will take time
everyone says it

I'm here to tell you that it's true
it will take time
to heal
to grow
to learn to love yourself above all others

allow yourself the time
to begin loving yourself

~ you are not hard to love

you hurt me
in the exact way you promised
you never would
but I could never hate you for it
no matter how much I try to convince myself

I do

this is the only life I've known
the only life I've lived

I don't know what to do
or how to do it right
but that's the thing

neither do you

so no matter how hard I try to hate you
I could never
because this is your first time living too

~ there's no blueprint

it wasn't until I was forced to sit with my own company
that I understood how easily I pushed the blame
onto myself
the truth is, I fought for you
for us

I pushed the blame onto myself
because I believed I wasn't enough
enough to be fought for
enough to be loved
enough for you to stay

the truth is, I fought for you
for us
it wasn't until you left the ring
when I noticed how bloody my knuckles were
and how yours were untouched

~ knockout

you must not allow another's actions
to make you question your value
you must remember
their actions are a reflection of them
your actions are a reflection of you

hurt people hurt people
I'd like to believe it's in our nature
because it would make the pain sting less

but they hurt you
and you didn't deserve it
so of course, it's going to sting
for days
months
maybe even years

and even though time heals
it will be hard
because you'll realize

you did not deserve it

~ *the best revenge*

letting go is difficult
especially if the person you're letting go of meant everything
but when has life ever been easy
we go through the biggest changes when faced with the hardest
obstacles
you may have to let them go because they didn't love you
in the way you deserve
you may have to let them go because you didn't love them
in the way they deserve
just because you let go
does not mean you couldn't hold on
it just means they weren't the right person
to hold on to

~ *not everyone is meant to stay*

when we were together
the lights seemed brighter
the grass seemed greener
the problems seemed smaller

I was so focused on the good
I didn't realize how much bad there was
until it was in front of my face

when I found myself having to live without you
my life began to crack down the middle
it was only when I took the time to look
I noticed it wasn't colorless

~ hidden geode

if you came back
crying and begging for me to give you one more chance

it's no lie that the girl I used to be
would have grabbed that chance
in a heartbeat
for I lost my home when you left

but you seem to forget
that girl I used to be
also sat there
on her knees
crying and begging for you to not leave

you can need me
but you were the one
who put yourself in a position to lose me

~ don't look back

after you did me dirty
you ran your mouth
the words flowing from your lips
were nothing but lies

after you did me dirty
I opened my mouth
the words flowing from my lips
were all the ones I had hidden away
when I was trying to protect the image of you

I protected you from the eyes of others
because I wanted them to see you in the way I did
not the way you actually were
I knew who you were
I knew how little you cared
but I convinced myself otherwise
just to be able to say

I'm loved
even if you didn't

~ respect yourself by leaving

you protected me
from the stares
as we walked down the street
hand in hand

you protected me
from the insults
as we browsed through the isles
arms linked

you protected me
from the thoughts that filled my mind
about what I deserved

you did protect me
to the best of your ability

but the one person
I wish you protected me from
was yourself

~ *a different kind of pain*

when you left
I racked my brain
to try and figure out why
crying to my sister
crying to my family
crying to my friends
simply to answer the question you left me with

no matter how many times I asked
they did not shut me down
or invalidate my feelings
they allowed me to grieve the loss
of best thing that has happened to me
they picked me up
when I did not have the strength to do it myself

and it was then I remembered
I am loved
with or without you there

~ unconditional

after we ended
people asked me
"why did you stay?"

the only answer I came up with was
I loved you
and I thought that was enough

it wasn't until I took the time
to look inside my heart
for me to understand
our love was not the same

I would never treat someone the way you did

~ *who we are*

the people that should love us
unconditionally

always hurt us the most

~ *blindsided*

if you want to turn around
and come back
claiming you miss me
please

don't

I don't miss the person I used to be
when you were here

~ leave like you once did

I would apologize
for not being enough
for you
but I am enough

for me

~ you don't define me

I'm not mad at you
for breaking my heart
or not knowing how to love me
in the same way I loved you
because I know
you needed the love I gave you
without having to return it

~ you deserve to be happy too

when I think back
I can see the moments we sat there
laughing at the little things
things we were sure to forget

we were in love
with one another
with life itself

when I think back
I begin to wonder
what was real
did you ever truly love me
or did you love the security I provided

because I still can't wrap my head around it

how do you intentionally hurt
the one you love
the way you did?

~ *unanswered questions*

from the moment we crossed paths
I grabbed my cup
and began pouring

         time

            effort

               trust

               love

into your

              cup

and it wasn't until
the last drop

    f

    e

    l

    l

that I realized I had nothing left
for myself

~ refills are unavailable

you asked me once
"what does love mean to you?"
and with a plethora of answers
the one I felt resonate with me
was that we were meant to grow together

not just literally
but figuratively too
as individuals
as lovers

we're meant to build off one another
and help our lover achieve their goals
while not forgetting about our own

love is the act of giving yourself to someone
while trusting them to handle you with care

we were carnations in a garden of roses
but you wilted
and left me to fend for myself

~ weeds

I was so scared of losing you
not because I didn't want to be alone
but all the love I had for you
no longer had a place to go

it was as if the faucet broke
and the water wouldn't stop pouring
from all the wrong places

it took time to fix it
to fix myself

I was so scared of losing you
not because I didn't want to be alone
but all the love I had in me
was never given to myself before

so when the water begins to pour
I won't allow myself to waste it

~ *fill your own bucket*

our choices lead us down different paths
yet when I look back,
I see you taking care of yourself
and pulling me along
disguising it as love
when in reality, I was your fall guy

~ along for the ride

longing for something that I knew was bad
felt natural
each time I answered your call
my life was unraveling
yet all I could do was sit there and watch

~ my monthly subscription

I wear my glasses to be able to see
the beauty in the world before me

but I was able to see
the beauty in you
without the help of artificial eyes

I was blinded by who you were
I didn't realize the truth of who you've become
until the frames sat on the bridge of my nose

~ things have become clear again

my culture claims I am unnatural
for who I choose to love
my religion claims it is a sin
for who I choose to love
my country claims I am not human
for who I choose to love

but I am finally happy
because of who I *chose* to love

~ shattering the stigmas

the moment the sun shines
I must face the problems that exist within my life
the ones that have accumulated

over   the   course   of   time

rise

to

begins

sun

the

as

the problems never truly disappear
and I would spend so much time on the *what if*
I never truly appreciated
what I had before it was gone

the heart longs for what it no longer has
too late to appreciate what I did not
becoming someone I was always meant to be
must be done

over   the   course   of   time

as

the

sun

begins

to

set

~ work of art

I sat there
confined to the prison you've locked me in
waiting behind the window
the wings we've created discarded in the corner
I wish my mind was protecting me
from putting my heart on the line
but it wasn't until I felt myself
falling through the air
that I realized
they must work in tangent

~ *Icarus*

if you couldn't give me your love
while we were together
I don't want your pity

you can keep it for yourself
since the only thing I lost
was a person who didn't love me

~ keep your hands to yourself

nature is quite a sight to behold
lost among us are the beauties of this world
the beauties hidden in the lakes, beaches, forests, earth, and sky
for a fleeting moment, we come to appreciate the vastness of it
but the moment was just that, fleeting
forgotten is Mother Nature

~ the value of life

the difference between who I am
and how people might see me
is vast

they do not know that I continue to see myself
as an author that cannot write
as a lover that cannot love
as a sister that cannot support
as a daughter that cannot invoke pride

as worthless

they do not know that I have stopped seeing myself as strong
enough

they may see me as intimidating
for it is easiest to push them away
before they get too close

they may see me as smart
for I spend every waking moment
reviewing all I have done
just to make sure it is good enough

they may see me as compassionate
yet they do not know that the only reason I have compassion
for those that do not have compassion for themselves
is because I wish someone would grant me that same relief

they may see me as being
joyful
content
understanding

but they do not know
what I see myself as

~ the chasm inside

you do not have to be perfect

you do not have to hide away
your feelings in the same way you hid
who you really are

you do not have to get a perfect grade
to prove that you are worthy
of your parents' love

it's enough that you're happy
with the choices you make
based on what you desire
for desire is the center of humanity,
and who has the right to strip you
of yours

you do not have to refrain
from experiencing love
simply to maintain an appearance

you are allowed to love another
while loving yourself

you must understand
you live with the choices you make

so no, don't give others the right to dictate your life

you do not have to be perfect

you can allow yourself to love
whomever you wish to love

even if all you want to start with is yourself

~ take the first step

you sit there
one on each side
always working
whether I'm suffocating you
with music
the sound of my lover's voice
or the voices in my own head
you continue to be there
without fail
without wavering

you allow me to find ways
to express myself
in the music that blasts through your canals
you sit there
one on each side
punctured just to look good

sometimes, I forget about you, but
the jewelry that decorates your body
allows me to remember that you exist

you sit there
one on each side
granting me a gift that some don't have
and for that
I am grateful you exist

~ *listen to the little things*

the bird falling from the sky
its wing, impaled

                              lo

                         ne
judgment — disappointment   li

                         ne

                    ss

the bright gold and red feathers shine brightly in the sun
lighting up the sky like a flaming meteor

its injuries keep it from taking flight
away from the people that had taken aim
its beauty brought stares of disapprovement
from those that could never compare
from those that don't understand
that differences are beautiful

regardless of the colors of my feathers
I am ready to take flight

~ from the ashes

we sit there
day after day
our faces glued to the screens that connect us around the world
and while we have the ability to be connected
we continue to choose to be divided

spewing hateful comments
believing we are protected
by the glowing brick
that rests in our hands
not realizing there's someone on the other end
someone real

~ say it to my face

you're confused
hurt
terrified
lost

I know

I would be lying if I said I wasn't

these feelings may be swarming within you
but don't give them the power to suffocate you

your power is yours alone
no one can take that away

~ *grab the reins*

to answer the question burning in people's mind
no
I don't wake up each day and choose to live in fear
walking down the street, watching over my shoulder
simply because of the person I'm walking next to
I can't choose who I'm attracted to
whether it be man or woman

what I can choose is if I follow my heart
so if I choose to love who I love
I'm choosing to be true to myself
I'm choosing to love me

~ my heart is set

people wish you well
praise you when you accomplish your goals
while hoping you fail
and focusing on your mistakes

if you continue to trip
they'll watch you fall
the whole way down
until they see that you can't get up
to try again

but that is when you must

~ the facade falls away

I get asked
"why don't you wear makeup?"

but what they don't understand is
I did the work I needed to do
to be able to love myself
despite my blemishes
without having to wipe off my face
each night before I go to sleep

that's not to say makeup is solely used so you can love yourself
but how am I supposed to
when I don't recognize the woman in the mirror

~ underneath the mask

we look at the stars
marveling at their beauty
as they shine in the black sky

yet, we don't allow ourselves the same grace

when we are surrounded by the dark
we do not look at how we shine
no matter how bright
instead we focus on when we flicker

just because the stars disappear
behind the clouds
does not mean they are any less beautiful

~ even when you don't shine

you are

enough for the late nights under the stars,
long drives with soft music
deep talks that may end in tears,
and everything that would come in between

the questions that flit about your mind,
making you question your worth,
should find their way to the exit,
for without you is a life I wish not to live

the small voice inside your head
that whispers your insecurities and flaws
couldn't be more wrong,
for we are our own greatest foes

if only you could love yourself
in the same way that I do,
you would appreciate the way
your eyes twinkle in the starlight

no artist has the ability to create a song
that would make me as content
as to when you perform
in the shower or car,

so if I have to spend the entirety of my life
reminding you of your worth,
then it is not a responsibility I will take lightly
because to put it simply:

we are enough,
my love

~ her

if you're looking for a sign
this is it:

let it go

no matter what it is
if it does not serve you
and what you wish to accomplish

let it go

I promise
you'll be okay.

~ free falling

I never understood the idea
we have free will
but our path is already known

no matter how long I pondered
it just never clicked
and maybe it never will
so instead of focusing on the why
it's best to focus on the how

the ending has no meaning
if the journey is not enjoyed

~ focus on what you can control

as humans
we are all so focused on the tragedies we face
believing they define us
and it's true

they do

but not to the extent we believe them to
they change us
to become stronger
so we can continue living another day

we focus on the pain they cause us
not the growth we went through

so while it's important to remember the tragedies
it's more important to not forget how we got through them

~ the beauty of growth

www.ingramcontent.com/pod-product-compliance
Lightning Source LLC
Chambersburg PA
CBHW051842040426
42447CB00006B/660